More Victorian Christmas

Coloring Fun

A Grayscale Adult Coloring Book

48 Vintage Coloring Pages

Grayscale Coloring Books

VOLUME 70

Vicki Becker

About the Author

Vicki Becker is an avid needlework enthusiast who loves everything arts and crafts! Mrs. Becker has been knitting and crocheting for over 48 years. She learned to crochet from her grandmother in the beautiful Adirondack Mountains of upstate New York where she grew up.

Mrs. Becker shares her knowledge and experience through her books with patterns for crochet, knitting, hand embroidery, and quilting. Vicki also enjoys making puzzle books, journals, and coloring books. She creates digital art, illustrations, and mixed media art for the designs in her books.

Vicki Becker lives in central Florida with her husband, four cats, and two dogs. Her hobbies include all forms of needlework, photography, digital art, cooking, and gardening.

What Is Grayscale Coloring?

Grayscale coloring means that you will be coloring over a black-and-white picture. The magic of coloring over grayscale is that the shading is already done for you! Even beginners with no knowledge of shading can achieve beautiful results. Colored pencils work beautifully with the grayscale images giving the finished picture depth and dimension. The paper is well suited for colored pencils but does not work as well with markers. If you use markers put a sheet of paper under the page in case of bleed-through.

ISBN-13: 978-1981577668

ISBN-10: 1981577661

First Printing, 2017
Printed in the United States of America

A Happy Christmas to you

Colorists Name

Date

Colorists Name

Date

A Merry Christmas to you

C. Reichert

Colorists Name

Date

A Bright and Happy Christmas to you

Colorists Name

Date

Christmas Greetings.

Colorists Name

Date

A Happy Christmas to you.

Colorists Name

Date

Colorists Name

Date

With Love and Merry Christmas Greetings From

Colorists Name

Date

A MERRY CHRISTMAS.

WITH FOND REMEMBRANCES AND ALL
GOOD WISHES FOR A BRIGHT CHRISTMAS.

Colorists Name

Date

A Happy Christmas to you.

Colorists Name

Date

Colorists Name

Date

Colorists Name

Date

Colorists Name

Date

A Merry Christmas

Colorists Name

Date

A happy Christmas

Colorists Name

Date

Colorists Name

Date

Colorists Name

Date

Colorists Name

Date

Colorists Name

Date

Colorists Name

Date

Colorists Name

Date

Colorists Name

Date

December
25
Christmas
Greetings

Colorists Name

Date

Colorists Name

Date

With Best Wishes for a Happy Christmas

Colorists Name

Date

CHRISTMAS GREETINGS.

Colorists Name

Date

Colorists Name

Date

A happy Christmas.

Colorists Name

Date

Best Christmas Wishes

Colorists Name

Date

Christmas Greetings

Colorists Name

Date

CHRISTMAS GREETINGS.

Colorists Name

Date

Merry Christmas Greetings.

Colorists Name

Date

A merry Christmas

Colorists Name

Date

A Happy Christmas to you

Colorists Name

Date

Colorists Name

Date

Colorists Name

Date

A Merry Christmas

Colorists Name

Date

Loving Christmas Greetings

Colorists Name

Date

TO WISH YOU A
HAPPY CHRISTMAS.

Colorists Name

Date

A Happy Christmas to you.

Colorists Name

Date

To Wish you a Happy Christmas

Colorists Name

Date

Colorists Name

Date

A
Happy
Christmas
to you.

Colorists Name

Date

Colorists Name

Date

December
25
A Happy
Christmas

Colorists Name

Date

Merry Christmas Greetings

Colorists Name

Date

A Merry
Christmas

HOME SWEET HOME

WARM
WISHES.

Made in the USA
Las Vegas, NV
17 February 2023

67662656R10057